The
American Dream
DECLASSIFIED

◆

Frank PN Adjei-Mensah

AuthorHouse™ LLC, 1663 Liberty Drive, Bloomington, IN 47403
www.authorhouse.com; Phone: 1-800-839-8640

First self-published Online in 2014 by: The American Dream
Declassified Limited

Cover designed by Daniel O Adjei-Mensah
Book Illustrations by: DAMKOS Artworks, England UK. Cover
illustration: mascot of the American Dream Declassified

Published by AuthorHouse 07/14/2014
ISBN: 978-1-4969-1490-3 (sc)
ISBN: 978-1-4969-1491-0 (hc)
ISBN: 978-1-4969-1466-8 (e)

Library of Congress Control Number: 2014909410

The
MASCOT

Frank P.N. ADJEI-MENSAH, BA (Hons, Law & Sociology) is a budding industrialist and Entrepreneur. He is an upstanding and active member of his community and a remarkable motivational speaker. He is also the author of American Dream Declassified KIDS Edition Volume I.

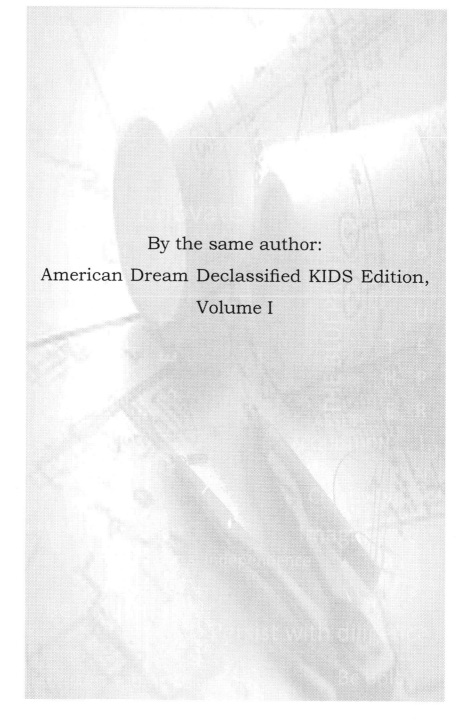

By the same author:

American Dream Declassified KIDS Edition,

Volume I

PROLOGUE

The Obama administration has made it more comfortable for people to go back to school to train or re-train for jobs, by expanding access to student loans. That is a serious thing, and many people have taken advantage of this incredible opportunity.

However, the income gap between the folks at the top and the rest of the population has widened even farther during this same period. Why? Meanwhile, except for the rich folks at the upper side, everyone else is feeling the financial squeeze in spite of their upgrades in education and career training. Why?

Student-loan bust is feared to be the next cause of financial collapse in the American economic system. Why? Why is it getting harder and harder for student loan borrowers to fulfil their repayment obligations, in spite of their wage and salary up ticks? Education is THE KEY to success, we've heard this over and over. What form of education are we talking about, though? Also, what sort of success are we expecting as a result? If financial success is EXPECTED, then financial education is REQUIRED.

While there are plenty of self-help books and DVDs from TV personalities and other "financial education gurus," most of these resources provide nothing more than teaching their patrons how to manage their money and get out of debt (i.e. how to manage poverty,) while they, on the other hand, focus their efforts on creating wealth for themselves.

Prepare yourself to be intrigued, as you read this easy-to-follow manual, for FINANCIAL SUCCESS.

CONTENTS

PREFACE

The American economic system is really generous to some folks, but to the financially struggling majority the cup seems always less than half full regardless of how hard they try. They earn college degrees, work hard at their jobs but still find themselves living from paycheck to paycheck. Many look up to the government and political leaders to help with the situation, but no such help seems forthcoming. Wall Street is no help either, and is thought to even contribute to the problem one way or some other. The harsh truth is that there is very little the government can do to avail at the individual or household level.

Some folks, notwithstanding, as noted earlier, are doing really well. What exactly do those people know that the rest of the struggling population don't? This book reveals the very blueprint of the American economic system down to its fundamental details, so that anyone can follow the principles and methods to acquire wealth and achieve the American Dream.

"It isn't sufficient just to want - you've got to ask yourself what you are going to do to get the things you want."

------Franklin D. Roosevelt

You will discover, as you read, that creating wealth is not as complicated as you might have imagined, and that explains why wealthy people are hardly the "smartest" or the "highly-educated."

I am a father, a husband, a nurse, an author, a student, and also an entrepreneur. Like most parents I want my kids to have better economic opportunities than I have. Like the Chinese proverb goes "It's better to teach someone how to fish, than to simply provide the fish." By implication, you have to know how to fish, before you can teach someone.

Haven had my fair share of financial struggles doing exactly what everyone else does, it dawned on me to research into why some people are doing so well in this economy while the majority of the population keep struggling. What do they know? What do they do differently? The results of the four-year-long research shocked me to my very core. I couldn't believe how uncomplicated it really is to create wealth and live the American Dream.

"Man's best successes come after their disappointments."

-----Henry Ward Beecher

For lack of knowledge, my people perish (Hosea 4:6.)

The economic pathways, passed on from generation to generation (i.e. go to school so you can get a safe and secured job with benefits and great pension plans) no longer apply favorably in this changed global economy.

Everybody needs financial education in addition to their degrees, diplomas, and professional training.

This book provides the entire financial education package you will ever need in a good or bad economy in an easy-to-understand step-by-step approach to wealth creation towards financial freedom.

While self-help books abound everywhere, I find major problems with most of them. The condescension they project is sickening, to say the least.

"Always bear in mind that your own resolution to succeed is more important than any other."

-------Abraham Lincoln

They teach you little more than learning how to manage your money (i.e. how to manage poverty.) They will lead you through mathematical and statistical projections that will help you pay off your debt in say ten to fifteen years, suggest you max-out your ROTH IRA contributions, get some 401K in place, and literary shrink yourself into a bottle by saving pretty much every dime you earn. These projections are based on a false sense of job security. In the unfortunate event of a job loss (which happens to millions of good people,) or some other mishaps that stop the paychecks, these extrapolations, like the "house of cards," come down to a screeching halt, along with all the hopes and dreams.

You become an efficient manager of poverty IF you succeed in going through the austerity measures they suggest to "help" you. Regrettably, you will NOT become wealthy after going through all that. What was the point then? The hypocrisy here is that those folks do not practice what they preach.

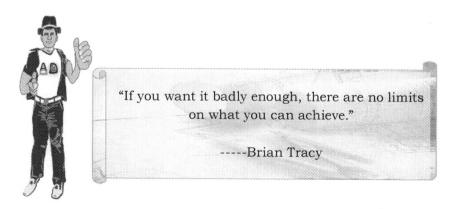

"If you want it badly enough, there are no limits on what you can achieve."

-----Brian Tracy

When they sit on TV and dispense these poverty-management ideas in their books and CDs, they are creating wealth for themselves, while they teach you how to manage poverty. Most of these folks do not have 401K, ROTH IRA, or practice what they advocate, and neither do they teach their kids to do same. They concentrate their efforts in creating wealth, and then hire professional accountants and money managers to manage their vast and ever-expanding wealth, and teach their kids to follow suit.

This book is for anyone willing and ready to modify their financial and economic fortunes for good. The primary target group, however, is the young children, for two main reasons; first, teach the child the way he should go so that he will not depart from it when he grows; second, old habits die hard. In addition to providing a thorough understanding of the American economy and easy-to-follow pathways to wealth creation, this book is also loaded with inspirational and motivational quotations from renowned leaders and sages.

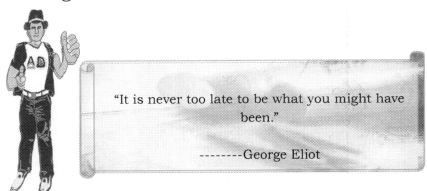

"It is never too late to be what you might have been."

--------George Eliot

The combined effect is bound to move the reader from knowledge into action. Inasmuch as my eight-year old son could read and understand the script, with a few explanations of some concepts by me, of course, and is excited about the prospects of his financial future, no one will remain the same after reading this book. My recommendation for readers is to go back and re-read the book a few times till the concepts and ideas become ingrained. Most importantly, have your kids do same if you have any. At that 'aha' moment, NOTHING can stop you from achieving the American Dream.

"Achievement seems to be connected with action. Successful men and women keep moving. They make mistakes, but they don't quit."
------Conrad Hilton

ACKNOWLEDGEMENTS

My sincere appreciation goes to God for the inspiration and energy provided to accomplish this project. To my wife Felicia and son Nigel I say thanks for the support and encouragement. To my brother Daniel (Foroza) I say thanks; you are a genius! To Rev. Ofosu-Addo, God bless you for your strong support and encouragement as well. To you (yes! You) the reader, I bid you good fortune as you gear up to claim your American Dream.

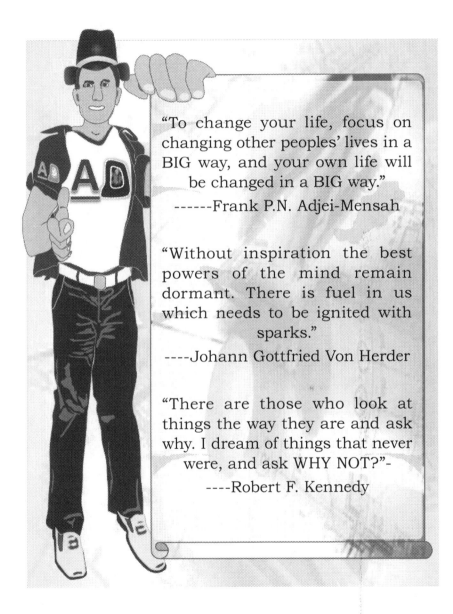

"To change your life, focus on changing other peoples' lives in a BIG way, and your own life will be changed in a BIG way."

------Frank P.N. Adjei-Mensah

"Without inspiration the best powers of the mind remain dormant. There is fuel in us which needs to be ignited with sparks."

----Johann Gottfried Von Herder

"There are those who look at things the way they are and ask why. I dream of things that never were, and ask WHY NOT?"-

----Robert F. Kennedy

PART ONE:

DEFINING THE AMERICAN DREAM

INTRODUCTION

The American economy works generously for some people, but not others, it is fair to say. The question is why does it work for some, but not for others? Do they know a secret that the rest of the struggling population does not?

This book provides the "blue print" for the basic understanding of how the American economy works, in such practical way that the average person can understand and implement the principles involved to turn their lives around from financial struggle for financial freedom.

Many people complain about the economy. It's difficult to find a job and keep it. Those with jobs still struggle to keep up with bills, and are only able to maintain just a basic livelihood. For many people the American Dream continues to be a fleeting unattainable fantasy.

"The key to happiness is freedom, and the key to freedom is courage".

------Kory Koontz

QUESTION: WHAT IS THE AMERICAN DREAM?

Lots of people I interviewed for this project understood the "American Dream" to mean having good-paying jobs with benefits and a good retirement account, having a house in a decent neighborhood, a nice car to get around, and being able to afford some moments of dining out with family, taking vacation trips etc.

To achieve this lifestyle, most people follow the same Industrial-Age economic script passed to them generations over, even though the economic landscape has shifted entirely. We tell our kids to go to school so they could get safe and secured jobs with benefits and great pension plans. The script ends there and so this is all they do, believing this will grant them the "American Dream" lifestyle they desire.

The reality is, with the changed economic landscape jobs are neither safe nor secure anymore.

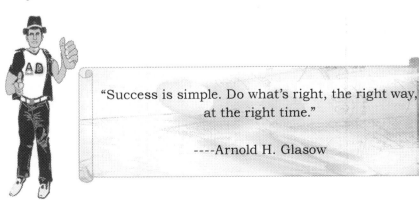

"Success is simple. Do what's right, the right way, at the right time."

----Arnold H. Glasow

Jobs which were hitherto thought to be secure can now be shipped overseas at a moment's notice, which sometimes affect entire industries, like the on-going outsourcing of manufacturing jobs to China.

When that happens, most folks go back to school to learn new skill-sets for jobs, hoping and praying that the new jobs will stick. Yet still, many people take to street demonstrations (Occupy Wall Street and all) calling on the government to "do something about it." The 99% Movement was born out of these frustrations. The cold truth is that, neither your employer, nor the government can solve this problem at the personal or household level without altering the basics of the American economy from capitalism to socialism, or communism at worse.

Socialism hasn't produced better economic results anywhere it has been tried. The collapse of the former Soviet Union attests to this fact.

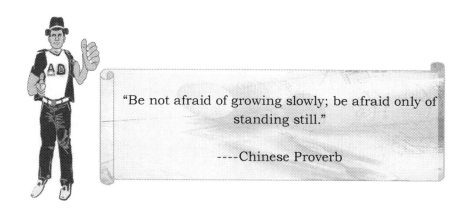

"Be not afraid of growing slowly; be afraid only of standing still."

----Chinese Proverb

Even communist countries like China, Russia and Cuba have all seen the enormous potentials in the capitalist economic model and are putting measures and structures in place to take advantage of this miraculous economic formulary. The bottom line is that, capitalism is here to stay.

In every economy there are three key players, namely; sellers of goods and services, buyers of such goods and services, and the system government in the middle as the referee setting the rules of the game and ensuring that the markets run smoothly and legally.

In the Capitalist free market such as the American economy, the government has an added responsibility to reward capitalists. It DOES NOT, and CANNOT reward labor at the same time, because if it does, then there will be no incentives for capitalists to take risks to produce goods and services needed by people.

"Unless you change how you are, you will always have what you've got."

-----Jim Rohn

The reward for the capitalists is twofold; profits, and tax incentives provided by the system governments. While these may sound simplistic, they are nonetheless the two most significant determining factors towards achieving financial freedom, and by extension the American Dream.

Governments at all levels; Federal, State, County, and City, rely heavily on capitalists to create jobs, goods, and services for everyone else.

In order to encourage capitalists to take risks and engage in these activities, these government entities provide tax credits and tax holidays.

They also maintain significantly lower taxes on profits. The United States is celebrated as "capitalists' heaven" for allowing capitalists to keep the bulk of their profits as opposed to others, like some European countries, where taxes on profits could be as high as 70% and over.

"Knowing is not enough; we must apply. Willing is not enough; we must do."

----Johann Wolfgang Von Goethe

Those countries tax capitalists heavily and use the tax proceeds to create social welfare programs to benefit those who are less economically fortunate. In the capitalist economy, on the other hand, the putative alliance is between capitalists and the government. Capitalists create jobs, goods, and services needed by people, they are then let off the hook tax-wise, literally.

The government then steps in to tax those they employ, as well as whoever purchases the goods and services they produce. Encouraging capitalists to engage in such economic activities is so crucial in keeping the economic engine running, that in some cases governments, even step in to absorb financial losses borne by capitalists.

Remember the bailouts in 2008, dubbed "Emergency Economic Stabilization Act of 2008?" In other words, profit is private, losses are public debt.

"The key to happiness is having dreams. The key to success is making your dreams come true."

-------Author Unknown

The wage-earner, on the flip side, is the proverbial "cash cow" ready to be milked every time he or she clocks in at the job. Overtime work engenders even more taxes as it pushes them into higher tax brackets.

Simply put, if all you have to supply to the market is your physical labor, skilled or unskilled, then brace yourself for financial struggle. On the other hand, if you are ready to transform your financial fortunes, then read on.

The answer to the question therefore is that "The American Dream" is about Freedom and the pursuit of Happiness. To live your life how you would like. Financial freedom is at the core of this self-emancipation.

In order to achieve and live the American Dream, the basic FORMULA used by ALL WEALTHY PEOPLE is to focus on acquiring and building up ASSETS. This does NOT necessarily mean you should strive to increase your PAYCHECK!

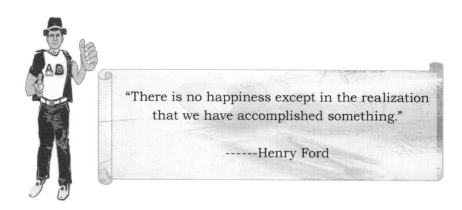

"There is no happiness except in the realization that we have accomplished something."

------Henry Ford

The Paycheck route is what the masses have been conditioned (not educated) to focus on, which is NOT A WINNING FORMULA, and explains why the masses keep struggling financially, in spite of pay raises.

THE BILLION DOLLAR QUESTIONS:

- What is an ASSET?

- What is a LIABILITY?

- What is the difference between an ASSET and a LIABILITY?
- What does it take to acquire ASSETS? (With or without money!)
- What does being WEALTHY really mean?

Understanding the above is ALL you need to become wealthy and live the American Dream. It is NOT COMPLICATED!

"Imagination is more important than knowledge."

--------Albert Einstein

That is why some people with very marginal academic and professional qualifications become wealthy, while other folks with PhDs, MBAs and other higher academic laurels keep struggling financially.

This project seeks to unpick this BASIC FORMULA apart to its fundamentals so that ANYONE, regardless of their current financial and academic status can follow and become FINANCIALLY WEALTHY and live the American Dream.

It will delve into various principles needed to transition successfully from the employee mindset to that of ownership. To think, behave and do what wealthy folks do.

This book is HIGHLY RECOMMENDED for ages nine (yes! 9) and above. Why so early? Two main reasons. First: Teach the child the way he should go, and when he is old, he will not depart from it. Second: Old habits die hard. More on these and other principles later in the book.

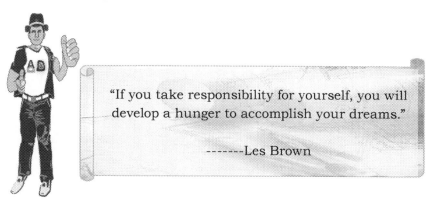

"If you take responsibility for yourself, you will develop a hunger to accomplish your dreams."

-------Les Brown

The disclosure: This is an attempt to de-classify the "American Dream" and any information obtained will be used for that purpose.

WHAT IS THE AMERICAN DREAM ABOUT?

The American Dream is about freedom and the pursuit of happiness. To spend your life in your own way without the saddle of financial constraints. What does this phraseology really mean? What does it suggest to you? What's in it for you?

You do not have to be a rocket scientist to understand that 'Financial Freedom' is at the very core of true freedom and, by extension, the American Dream. The seemingly elusive question is; what constitute financial freedom? Most importantly, how can you achieve financial freedom?

When you work for a paycheck, would you consider that as having financial freedom?

"We can have more than we've got because we can become more than we are."

----Jim Rohn

If you could be fired or lose that job for whatever reason cited by your employer, would you still reckon you have financial freedom?

When your income would stop coming in if you suffer some debilitating illness, and become incapable of working, would you still consider yourself as having financial freedom just because you have a job?

It is obvious that simply having a great job does not inevitably mean that you have achieved financial freedom, and by extension The American Dream.

Financial freedom means having your money, your ideas, other people, and systems work for you rather than you working for money. Work becomes a choice, not a need. Meaning you get to choose what to do with your time, either to work or not to work. At that level, you are considered "wealthy."

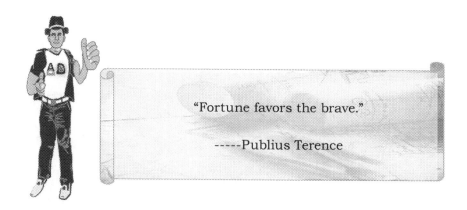

"Fortune favors the brave."

-----Publius Terence

"Men do less than they ought, unless they do all they can."

-----Thomas Carlyle

"What the mind can conceive and believe, it can achieve."

-----Napoleon Hill

"Who aims at excellence will be above mediocrity; who aims at mediocrity will be far short of it."

------Burmese Saying

"Plans are nothing; planning is everything."

----Dwight D. Eisenhower

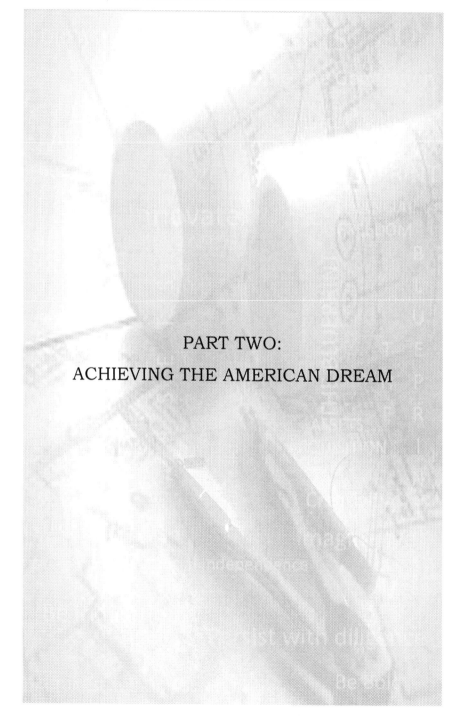

PART TWO:

ACHIEVING THE AMERICAN DREAM

WHAT DOES BEING WEALTHY REALLY MEAN?

Being wealthy, as opposed to being "rich" has to do with how long you can live, survive, thrive, and even improve your standard of living if for any reason you cannot work or decide not to work. It does not necessarily stand for how much money you have in the bank, it is instead about how you earn a living. Specifically, it is about having your money work for you, rather than you working for money.

Apart from old-age and infirmity, there are various reasons why people may decide not to work at a job. Fun is one significant reason. Being wealthy means that you have successfully out-sourced your income-generating processes outside of yourself. You spend very little or no time on your own in generating your income. In other words, you don't have to be physically involved continuously in the income-generating process.

"Success is to be measured not so much by the position that one has reached in life as by the obstacles which he has overcome."

-------Booker T. Washington

This then affords you the free time to do whatever else you desire, including doing things for fun wherever and whenever. Spending more time with family and friends, raising your children, volunteering your time for charitable endeavors, helping others, traveling around the world are all significant and motivating reasons for becoming wealthy.

Being able to bequeath to your children and family, such income generating systems ranks among the top most motivating factors why people strive to become wealthy.

With the freed-up time, many wealthy folks find other lucrative ventures to engage in, and generate even more wealth. These wealth-creating activities soon become a habit, and explains why wealthy people keep getting wealthier. On the flip side, the activities that financially struggling people engage in also become a habit that results in more financial struggles, until they change those habits.

"Many of life's failures are people who did not realize how close they were to success when they gave up."

-------Thomas Edison

Harnessing the worthy and discarding those unfavorable habits has been among the principal objectives of this book project.

WHAT DOES BEING RICH MEAN, AS OPPOSED TO BEING WEALTHY?

The basic difference between the two has to do with how the income is generated. If you win a large amount on the lottery, you will be considered rich, but not necessarily wealthy. If your paycheck gross in the millions annually, you may be considered very rich, but yet again, not necessarily wealthy. Being wealthy is determined by three benchmarks:

The direction of your net cash flow: If there is more money flowing into the account than flowing out of it, wealth is being built. On the other hand, if there is less or no money flowing into the account than out of it, wealth is not accumulating or being built.

"First say to yourself what you would be; then do what you have to do."

-----Epictetus

It is only a matter of time before the money in the account runs out, which explains why a good number of lottery winners go broke eight years afterwards.

How the income is generated: Those who rely solely or heavily on their paychecks, regardless of the size, are at an increased risk of financial meltdown in the event of professional accident or other unforeseen events that result in their inability to earn a living, when the paycheck stops.

Many hitherto high-earning athletes like boxers, footballers, basket-ball players, etc., suffer similar fate financially. Alas, the majority of the population is in the same boat, relying solely or heavily on paychecks.

Whether or not the wealth could be passed on to the next generation: If your income is generated solely from earned paychecks you could be considered rich if the checks are large enough.

"Every ceiling, when reached, becomes a floor, upon which one walks as a matter of course and prescriptive right."

-------Aldous Huxley

However, since you cannot pass on your professional performance to your next-of-kin, you will not be considered wealthy in spite of the large paychecks. On the other hand, if you were to set up income-generating system which runs with or without your physical day-to-day input, this could be passed on to your next-of-kin.

The next question begging to be asked is: What Can I Do to Become Wealthy? Before we answer this principal question, let's examine the parts played by savings and jobs in wealth creation.

THE ROLE OF SAVINGS IN WEALTH CREATION

If you are a fun of the so-called "financial gurus" on television, then you are familiar with the phrase "save money." The same phrase has been used by advertisers in various commercials for decades.

"There are two primary choices in life: to accept conditions as they exist, or accept the responsibility for changing them."

--------Denis Waitley

Sometimes I marvel if the term "save money" is reckoned to be a panacea for wealth creation and, by extension, the magic wand for achieving the American Dream. The truth is that saving money alone is NOT enough to achieve the American Dream. For the average American household with an annual income of about $50K, how long will it take to save enough to be considered wealthy?

Meanwhile, remember that being wealthy is NOT about how much money you have in the bank. Rather, as you read earlier, it's about how long you can survive if you cannot work for whatever reason, or you chose not to work at a job any longer and still be able to maintain and even improve your standard of living.

The "SAVE MONEY" mind-set has come to supplant the "CREATE VALUE" mind-set, the very cornerstone of the capitalist economic model. "Save money" could be a smokescreen which blinds folks from really seeing the bigger picture.

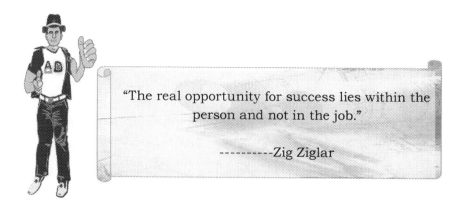

"The real opportunity for success lies within the person and not in the job."

----------Zig Ziglar

Capitalists create value and get rewarded for their efforts. In many cases the reward continues to pour in long after the original value creator has passed away. Their families continue to enjoy the benefits of such creations from generation to generation. This is what being wealthy means. This is the American Dream.

CAUTION!! None of the above explanations should be misconstrued to mean that saving money is bad. In fact, you cannot become wealthy if you cannot save money. If you consume every income you earn, your resources will soon dry out. What I'm saying is that saving money alone is not the manner to create wealth. The money needs to work to make even more money.

By the way, most commercials lure folks to spend money under the guise of saving money, just beware.

"We are persuaded to spend money we don't have on things we don't need to create impressions that won't last on people we don't care about."

--------Tim Jackson

THE ROLE OF JOBS IN WEALTH CREATION

Jobs! Jobs!! Jobs!!! Turn on the television or radio and start counting how many times you hear politicians and news anchors mention the word "jobs" in a 10-minute time span.

The problem I find with that chorus is the relatively exclusive under-tone of encouraging folks to seek jobs by obtaining college degrees.

They sound as though the only way to make it in this economy is by obtaining college degree(s) to land a job, when there is ample evidence of folks with college degrees working for minimum wage or something close to that. The result is a glut of college-degree holders chasing non-existing jobs, and not enough job creators.

What happened to creativity and imagination? Albert Einstein said "imagination is more important that knowledge."

"Success often comes to those who have the aptitude to see way down the road."

------Laing Burns, Jr.

In 2013, a high school student in England designed an App called "SUMMLY" which Yahoo reportedly purchased for $30 million.

The question is, what were all those with PhDs in software design employed at Yahoo, Google, Microsoft, etc., doing? The answer? They, too, are products of the "job" mentality. Most people go to work and use very little or no active imagination and creativity at all. They must follow regulations of the job or professional practice. They dare not "spin out of control" and utilize their own imagination instead of sticking to rules. Does the phrase "use it or lose it" sounds familiar?

For outliers like Steve Jobs, Bill Gates, Mark Zuckerberg etc., the quest to use their imagination instead of being "boxed-in" is the most important driving force which propelled them to those heights and set them financially free in the process.

"Great spirits have always encountered violent opposition from mediocre minds."

------Albert Einstein

In this Information Age era, it is even more important and imperative to challenge and encourage your kids to nurture their active imaginations and creativity for two main reasons: Firstly, because the financial rewards could be astronomical. Secondly, because there are more tools and resources available to them now than ever before to turn their creativity and imaginations into financial success. This is the era of the internet, social networking, and crowd-funding, all in a global village.

THE NEW REALITY OF JOBS FROM HISTORICAL PERSPECTIVE

The need to overhaul the education system to address the new realities of global economics has never been more relevant and urgent. To forge ahead and continue to prosper, we need to educate and ingrain this new approach and understanding of the American Dream compellingly and NOW!

"The future belongs to those who believe in the beauty of their dreams."

--------Eleanor Roosevelt

Folks heed the advice of their parents and the government to earn college degrees, land jobs of their dreams, then when all seem sorted the industries are outsourced with the jobs. They then flock back to school to re-train for new jobs and industries.

The cycle goes on and on till they retire, IF they can afford to retire. They simply TRAIN to supply their labor to the market, as opposed to being CULTIVATED to take advantage of the real provisions and applications of capitalism.

The United States ranks among the lowest in percentage of entrepreneurs, a mere 7.2%. This should not make anyone proud. My humble suggestion is for education authorities to incorporate financial education (should be more than just entrepreneurship training) into degree and professional training programs.

"Once you say you are going to settle for second, that's what happens to you in life."

------John F. Kennedy

This will help ensure that students don't just graduate and queue up for jobs, but could alternatively use their knowledge and skills acquired to create value in goods and services of their own, create assets.

This is sure to bring out the untapped creative energies lying dormant in most students and professionals, and encourage them to take charge to become financially independent. This is the most certain path to bring down and maintain low unemployment levels across board for the long haul.

The American economic system, and by extension the global economy, cycles between booms and busts. For countless decades, the economy recovered almost fully from busts shortly after the government puts stimulating measures in place. The recession that began in 2007, however, seems to linger on for much longer than expected, why? The answer is rooted in an important major periodic economic displacement of labor.

"You don't become enormously successful without encountering and overcoming a number of extremely challenging problems."

-------Mark Victor Hansen

The Industrial Revolution, which begun sometime around the 1760s ushered in a new manufacturing process from hand production methods to machines. While it brought major advances in the production processes, and in the standard of living of the masses, labor had to switch from raw hand skills to machine operation. Labor had to learn new skills.

The Agricultural Revolution, which occurred between the 15th century and the 19th century, also saw major improvement in food security and agricultural productivity. There again, it necessitated the displacement of over 90 percent of agricultural labor, which were absorbed into the manufacturing and other industries.

With the unceasing advancement in manufacturing technology and increased productivity, labor, again, had to switch from the factory floor to information processing in customer service line of work etc.

"One secret of success in life is for a man to be ready for his opportunity when it comes."

-----Benjamin Disraeli

The Information Age then arrived with the birth of the computer and the internet, bringing national economies together into one giant global economic village. All the world economies of substance have fully embraced this new reality. Goods and services tend to be produced in the most economically viable and cheapest locations on the globe.

This simply means that if something can be manufactured with less production cost in say China or India as compared to America, then the factory will be re-located to those countries.

Recent phenomena indicate that this transformation is not going to be limited to the production of physical goods only, but services as well. Airline companies are now using repair facilities in other countries and paying much less than they would in the USA.

Customer service jobs are also being outsourced to India, The Philippines etc. The list could go on and on.

"If you don't like something, change it. If you can't change it, change your attitude."

-----Maya Angelou

The healthcare industry, which is considered by many as the final frontier that cannot be outsourced elsewhere is now experiencing the very opposite of that prognosis.

Entrepreneurs in India, Brazil and other countries are building hospital facilities comparable, and in some instances far more advanced in technology and service delivery than the average hospital in America, for much less cost to the patient. This is driving up a boom in healthcare tourism to those countries and it's only a matter of time before these phenomena pick up steam in Mexico. Once that happens, healthcare cost in America would plummet significantly, along with wages and salaries in the industry.

Folks in the healthcare industry have already noticed a glut in labor supply and stagnating wages. Sign-on bonuses are just about a thing of the past.

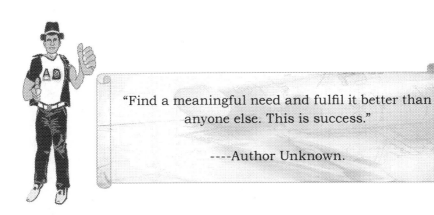

"Find a meaningful need and fulfil it better than anyone else. This is success."

----Author Unknown.

Campus recruitment of professionals, like nurses, has just about disappeared too, but yet schools that popped-up overnight to train these professionals keep churning out more fresh hands, exacerbating the glut and depressing wages even further.

The Obama Administration has made it more accessible and compelling for folks to go back to school to upgrade or obtain new skills for new jobs, and many people have responded affirmatively to the call in an attempt to close the income gap. The results, however, have proven otherwise. The income gap has widened even farther during this same period, how come? Well, with new career skills, more folks have either joined the labor force, causing a drop in the unemployment levels, or have seen some upticks in their wages from upgraded career and professional skill.

The combined results is that more people have experienced some increased purchasing power to shop for goods and services.

"The successful always has a number of projects planned, to which he looks forward. Any one of them could change the course of his life overnight."
-----Mark Caine

This in turn has caused over 90% of the gains of the economic recovery to accrue to the top 1% which own big businesses that produce these goods and services.

Folks with new or upgraded skills, on the other hand, are saddled with more student loans and increased taxes, causing a financial squeeze on their budgets. Student loan default is on the ascent, and is feared to be on a trajectory to cause the next financial bubble-bust in the American economic system.

When folks don't know what to do, they simply resort to what everyone else does. The problem is that everyone else is struggling financially, with the exception of the few who are doing really well in the economy. Those few are the capitalists. To do well like them, you have to learn their ways and teach same to your kids. If not, the cycle of financial struggle will pass along to the next generation as though "that's just the way it is" by default. It really shouldn't!

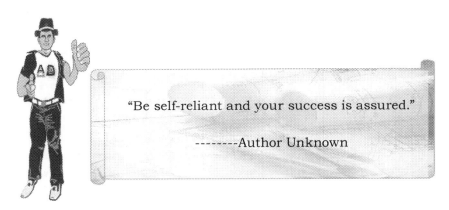

"Be self-reliant and your success is assured."

--------Author Unknown

Simply put, if you do what everyone does, you will end up having what everyone have, which is a financial struggle for the masses, and economic prosperity for the few capitalists. Understanding the ways of the capitalists is what this book project is about.

Capitalists focus on solving problems, not necessarily of their own, but of the masses, and get financially rewarded handsomely. They sniff around to discover problems that affect the masses. The bigger the problems the greater the rewards.

In many instances, the capitalist even enlists the services of professionals and technical folks to come up with the solution to the problem. The capitalist then takes the credit and the lion's share of the rewards, while everyone else gets their paychecks.

"If you do not change direction, you may end up where you are heading."

-----Lao Tzu

ADDRESSING THE WIDENING INCOME INEQUALITY

Education is THE KEY to success. What form of education, and what sort of success are we referring to? Doctors go to medical schools, nurses attend nursing schools, and police officers attend training schools to prepare them to be successful in their various drills. None of the training modules for these and other professions guarantee financial success.

The widening income gap in America has nothing to do with inadequacy of skills or training, or shortage of professionals thereof. In fact, it's quite the contrary.

Globalization has resulted in American workers fiercely competing among themselves, as well as with workers everywhere else on the globe. In other words, there's a larger pool of qualified workers available for employers to choose from now than ever before.

"Failures do what is tension relieving, while winners do what is goal achieving."

-----Dennis Waitley

The deck is stacked heavily against American workers, because even though it's a globalized economy, yet students in developing countries like China, India, Malaysia, etc. do not have to pay as much college tuition as American students. They can, therefore, afford to take much lower wages and salaries.

Capitalists are the net beneficiaries of this global superstructure, and they are cashing in BIG. Employers don't have to increase wages and salaries to attract qualified workers when they have enough to choose from.

This is one reason why the income gap is widening. The larger the pool of qualified workers, the wider the income gap becomes. In healthcare, hospitals are looking for ways to reduce costs while still providing quality care. They are now requiring RN nurses to have Bachelor degrees, mostly without a corresponding bump in the wage rate, more student loans accrue, however.

"I believe that the true road to preeminent success in any line is to make yourself master of that line."

-------Andrew Carnegie

Nursing Boards in many states are also requiring Nurse Practitioners to have Doctorate degrees, largely without any bump in the wage rate either, but again more student loans accrue. NPs with doctorate degrees can do most things doctors do, for less wage. In other words, these boards are creating quasi doctors out of nurses. This will bring down the demand for doctors, along with their wages and salaries.

The solution to the widening income gap is not necessarily to reverse globalization. The solution rests squarely with labor. Labor needs to discover and do what capitalists do. If you can't beat them, join them.

Learn to create assets to increase your prospects of getting off the labor grid. That calls for financial education, which is what you are getting from this book. Financial education isn't necessarily about learning how to manage your money or become an entrepreneur. It's about learning how to create money from ideas, which is what those at the top do.

"The best way to find yourself is to lose yourself in the service of others."

---Mohandas Gandhi

Billionaires don't make billions by saving money. They make billions by creating money; creating value in goods and services, mostly by applying their creativity and imaginations. They utilize the core principles of capitalism. It will help a great deal if this was taught in schools right from 1st grade, the ONLY WAY to level the playing field.

IF MONEY WASN'T AN ISSUE WHAT WOULD YOU DO WITH YOUR TIME?

Most people I surveyed for this project responded they would spend more time with family and friends, travel around the world, volunteer their time for church and charity works, spend more time at the gym, spend more time raising and nurturing their kids etc. What is stopping them is money, or is it?

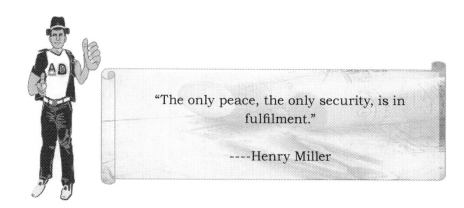

"The only peace, the only security, is in fulfilment."

----Henry Miller

For a good number of people, what is really stopping them from living the life of their dreams, is NOT money per se, rather HOW they earn the money.

When asked if folks would work 8 hours each day, five days a week for a $20k monthly paycheck, or would rather prefer half of that income earned from assets which require little of their own personal time? Each and every one of the respondents preferred the latter, assets.

Food, and food-in-a-trap are not the same. When you spot food in a trap and you go for it, you may eat the food alright but could get entrapped. What good was the food to you then? This is the plight that separate wealthy folks from everyone else, including even those who are simply rich but not wealthy. Consider sportsmen like footballers, boxers, etc., while they earn substantial incomes in the millions annually, they are just one professional accident away from financial ruins if the bulk of their income comes from their vocation.

"A wise man will make more opportunities than he finds."

--------Francis Bacon

They, like most wage/salary earners, live according to their income. Their incomes go up, so do their expenditures. Any unforeseen adverse event ushers them into financial ruins.

I could go on and cite many famous sportsmen and entertainers who have fallen on financial dire straits. After the high life they kick and scream into the company of over 70% of Americans either broke or living from paycheck to paycheck.

Once more, the size of your income matters LESS than HOW the income is earned when it comes to wealth creation. Those who earn their income solely from paychecks soon max-out their earning potentials. To increase their income, the beaten pathway is to go back to school to earn more degrees, which also entails more student loans and increased taxation as they enter into higher tax-brackets.

Those who earn their incomes from assets are treated much more favorably by the government in tax incentives.

> "The great thing in this world is not so much where we stand, as in what direction we are moving."
>
> ------Oliver Wendell Holmes

Their actions create jobs, goods and services. They are the capitalists. They get rewarded to encourage more of those activities.

Food in a trap values less than food in the wild. Food in a trap, like a job and paycheck, can still be very tempting. It can even blind you from discovering the trap, because most traps are designed to be less obvious.

Someone on his way to a job interview bumped into a brilliant business idea that could earn him millions. He simply brushed it aside and headed for the interview, thinking that in a month or less he will ensure a paycheck as opposed to taking risks even if the business idea sounds plausible. This is the by-product of the "jobs" mind-set.

Society needs professionals of every category; Doctors, nurses, police officers, teachers, truck drivers, firefighters and what have you. The aim of this book is NOT to discourage readers from the pursuit of their beloved professions and careers. Far from that, actually.

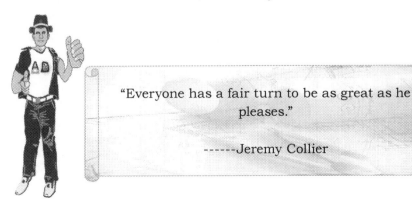

"Everyone has a fair turn to be as great as he pleases."

------Jeremy Collier

In fact, sensible and reasonable college degrees and professional qualifications are highly encouraged. After all, the sense of pride and accomplishment that comes with academic and professional achievement is priceless.

The single most significant goal of this book as a project is to set people financially free regardless of their academic and professional backgrounds and pursuits. To help folks achieve the seemingly elusive American Dream.

Most people love their profession and chosen career pathways. They are glad with the contributions and differences they make in society. The problem is money and time. The solution is ASSETS.

If assets are bringing in the bulk of your income, you are, nevertheless, free to practice your profession except, this time, ON YOUR TERMS.

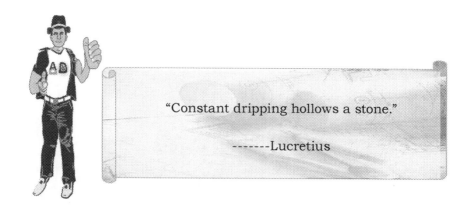

"Constant dripping hollows a stone."

-------Lucretius

You can choose when and where you work (if you decide to work), take vacation trips, spend quality time with family whenever you desire. Assets are the key to realizing the American Dream, perhaps the only key.

WHAT IS AN ASSET?

Asset, the single most important, but misunderstood, word which caused the fiscal meltdown of the American economy and, by extension, the global economy in 2007/2008.

For the purpose of wealth creation, an Asset would be defined as anything that generate income regularly, continuously, legally and does not require the owner's continuous physical presence for the purpose of such income generation. In other words, assets generate income and increases the owner's bank balance regularly, say monthly, without demanding the owner to be continually involved in the income-generation process.

"The great use of life is to spend it on something that will outlast it."

---William James

The definition is embedded with some pointers regarding what counts as an asset.

First of all, an asset must be something that adds or increases your bank account balance regularly, rather than induce a net decrease in the bank balance.

Secondly, a true asset does not call for the physical presence of the specific owner for the purpose of generating income. This implies that an asset would generate income with or without the physical presence of the owner.

THE MYTH ABOUT A HOUSE AS AN ASSET

At the mention of the word "asset" the first thing most people instinctively think about is a house or landed property. However, the house that you purchased to live in will NOT be considered an ASSET.

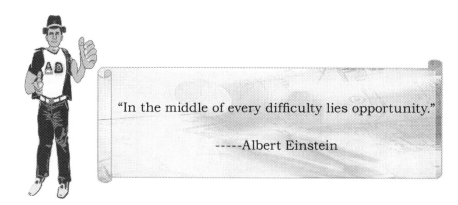

"In the middle of every difficulty lies opportunity."

-----Albert Einstein

The misunderstanding of this fact is the single most significant cause for the crash of the American economy in 2007/2008.

Many people are still convinced that their residential houses are assets. Their realtors, mortgage officers, and financial advisors keep telling them so. They are made to believe that, the bigger the house you purchase the bigger your asset, and the better off you are.

As a consequence of this gross misunderstanding some home buyers rush off to buy big houses and stretch their budgets thin trying to pay for it. Even when their income levels would not qualify them for Mortgage on such large houses, their mortgage brokers would maneuver and pull all the strings in their professional arsenal to "help" them acquire the houses of their dreams. The new homeowners are delighted with such brilliant efforts on the part of the brokers, little do they know that they had just been "helped" to dig their own financial "graves."

"Nothing can stop the man with the right mental attitude from achieving his goal; nothing on earth can help the man with the wrong mental attitude."
--------Thomas Jefferson

The fact that the house will not increase their bank balance mean that it would not necessarily help them accumulate wealth. The myth that the value of a house always goes up, which is supposed to serve as a justification for acquiring larger houses was made clear in the collapse of the housing bubble in 2007. After the collapse, the "American dream houses" became nightmares that everyone was walking or running away from.

The problem is that, because many people still do not understand the root cause of the housing collapse, they are heading back to feed around the same troughs where they got "slaughtered" not long ago. The bubble WILL inflate again, and bust again and again until homebuyers come to grasp with what that whole transaction really represent to their financial bottom line. A residential home is actually a LIABILITY, because it drains the bank account balance of its owner more than it increases on a monthly basis with mortgage interest tax deductions.

"Every day do something that will inch you to a better tomorrow."

----Doug Firebaugh

Even when a home is fully paid off, it remains a property, NOT AN ASSET. It still needs maintenance, updating, heating, cooling, real estate taxes, and so on, all of which cost money and therefore cause a reduction in your bank account balance, NOT an increase.

This does not necessarily imply that you should not buy a home. For the same reason you will not purchase a semi-truck for the purpose of daily commute due to high gasoline mileage, you should simply be mindful of the fact that a house will drain your bank account, and that the bigger the house the higher the financial drainage on the account.

A house, like most properties, can become a true asset and bring income and thus help build wealth if it is rented out and has positive cash flow. In other words, if it generates excess income and contribute to increasing your bank account, say at the end of the month after all expenses on the house are taken care of, then it is an asset.

"Choice, not circumstances, determines your success."

-----Author Unknown

The more of these assets you have the most wealth you are accumulating, and the better off you are towards achieving the American Dream.

In the same vain, a property like a car or truck could be worked into an asset for the purpose of wealth creation when you convert them into commercial usage.

This implies that as long as these are put to strictly private use, they are simply properties, NOT assets for the purpose of wealth creation.

I must emphasize here again that, none of the reasoning above should be misconstrued to mean that buying a house is bad. Far from it. Everyone needs a roof over their heads, and in many instances you are better off if you own rather than rent. However, if your aim is to increase your wealth, common sense dictates that you must trim your expenses alongside.

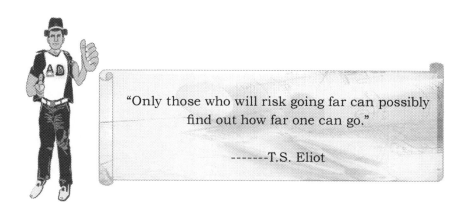

"Only those who will risk going far can possibly find out how far one can go."

-------T.S. Eliot

This means that you must NOT purchase more house than you need, the same way you do not buy a semi-truck for daily commute. When you purchase more house than you genuinely need, those who benefit the most are the government in higher real estate taxes, the realtor in larger commissions, and the mortgage loan officer also in larger commissions.

Your portion of the transaction is: more fun and space (needed or not), larger mortgage payment, more house maintenance expenses, more real estate taxes, and the hope that the value may go up to produce equity, which does not always happen- a gamble at best and a nightmare in the worst case scenario, as occurred in 2007/2008.

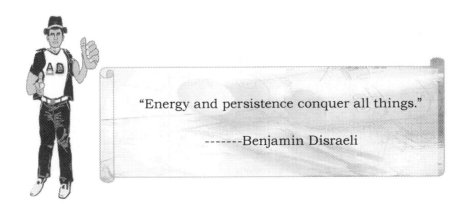

"Energy and persistence conquer all things."

-------Benjamin Disraeli

WHAT DOES IT TAKE TO ACQUIRE ASSETS AND CREATE WEALTH? (WITH OR WITHOUT MONEY!)

As discussed earlier, assets simply add money consistently and periodically to your bank account, whereas liabilities take money from your bank account consistently and periodically.

Assets are the cornerstones of wealth. The more assets you have, the wealthier you are. Liabilities, on the other hand, are the cornerstones of poverty. The more liabilities you have, the poorer you are, all things being equal. If there is any single word you must remember from reading this book, it is ASSET!

I cannot stress this enough. If you have money, buy assets. If you do not have money, then create assets.

"When love and skill work together, expect a masterpiece."

------John Ruskin

The majority of Americans lives from paycheck to paycheck. Transitioning from this check-to-check living to becoming wealthy is exactly what inspired the authorship and publishing of this book. The question is, how do you create assets with nearly no money? The following eight steps will help you create assets and wealth:

1. You must understand how the capitalist economy works, which was discussed earlier in detail in the introduction part. This is very important because lots of people study and understand only part of the economy and miss the bigger picture, but it is crucial that they study and understand the bigger picture and the roles played by the various parts.

Let's consider the role of the stock market, for example. If people understood the bigger economic picture, they would not rush off to buy stocks backed by corroded real estate derivatives and lose their investments.

"As a rule, he who has the most information will have the greatest success in life."

------Benjamin Disraeli

DO NOT INVEST IN SOMETHING YOU DO NOT UNDERSTAND OR HAVE ZERO CONTROL OVER! If you do, you are, in many ways, simply gambling.

2. You must understand and appreciate the difference between an asset and a liability, and concentrate on creating or acquiring more assets alongside limiting your financial obligations. This was likewise discussed in detail earlier.

If a property puts money in your pocket periodically and consistently, it is an asset. Acquire more and more of those, and you are building wealth. On the other hand, if a property takes money out of your pocket consistently and periodically, it is a liability. Acquire less of those. Not complicated!

3. While there are various categories and classes of assets, you must consider which class or categories best fit your personal interest.

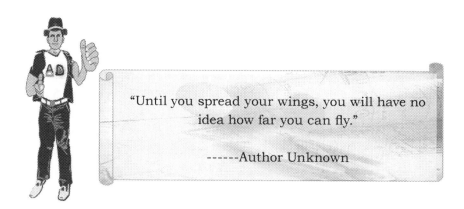

"Until you spread your wings, you will have no idea how far you can fly."

------Author Unknown

You must weigh the risks and benefits associated with those assets. Bear in mind that we are in the Information Age, so choose your assets wisely with this economic era in mind.

While some remnants of Industrial Age ideas still linger on, you would be better off looking into Information Age ideas for various reasons, including the relatively less initial capital outlay involved.

J.K. Rowling, the lady who authored the "Harry Potter" books and movies was reportedly a single mother on welfare. The book series has since made her a multi-billionaire. Mark Zuckerberg of Facebook, Bill Gates etc. are all cases in point of the unprecedented opportunities the Information Age has to offer.

Kids return from school, finish their homework and bear down on video games. My advice here is for parents to nurture and actively encourage their children's imagination and creativity on the home-front.

"There is only one success.... to be able to spend your life in your own way."

------Christopher Morley

Challenge them to reach beyond their academic and professional goals. To actively use their creativity and imagination to create assets.

In 2013, CNN reported of a high school student who turned roughly $700 into $250 million in three years. She had apparently saved about $360 from babysitting, and when her parents advised that she comes up with a business idea to help pay for a car when she turns 15 the next year, she stated "I brainstormed to see what I can do."

She came up with the thought of homemade custom jewellery with a match-up initial capital from her parents. It is just astonishing what people can do when encouraged to use their creativity and imagination.

4. You must consider your current financial status. As indicated earlier, if you have money buy assets. If you don't have money, then create assets.

"Take calculated risks. That is quite different from being rash."

------George S. Patton

You must weigh your current economic status, and if you are like most struggling Americans, then the way out of that vicious cycle is to tap into your creativity and imagination. Systems, like the internet and the ever-expanding social media are vital resources which could be harnessed to help create wealth.

5. You must consider or build up your mental capabilities as well as managerial abilities. A business or scheme that brings in money consistently and regularly with or without the physical presence of the owner is considered an asset. Take into account your managerial shrewdness, mental and emotional competences when deciding on such elaborate ventures you will like to engage, while not underestimating your strengths.

"The difference between a successful person and others is not lack of strength, not lack of knowledge, but rather a lack in will."

----Vince Lombardi

Bear in mind too, that if it requires your physical presence continuously in order to function, it means you have employed yourself, and the establishment would not be considered a true asset that provides financial independence. Your ultimate goal, which is to achieve the American Dream, is to become financially independent, even of your own self.

Assets raking in the money with little or no physical presence on your part on a continuous basis is what you should aim for. This is the financial secret of the wealthy, which sets them free from financial worries, so they can enjoy life their way. Some of these assets keep generating incomes even when the owners are asleep or incapacitated.

6. You must consider the diverse resources and systems you already have at your disposal. Carefully evaluate your available resources and figure out which pathway would provide the most benefits for you and your family now and future generations as well.

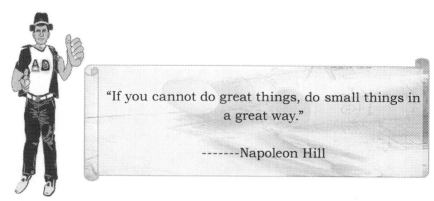

"If you cannot do great things, do small things in a great way."

-------Napoleon Hill

Let's suppose you are a teenager still living with your parents and do not have anyone financially dependent on you.

In this case you can afford to be more adventuresome and consider risks in your pursuits than someone with family to provide for, in which case they must transition perhaps slowly and cautiously to avoid unwanted financial casualties.

7. You must study the market you are trying to serve. Conduct an active inquiry into the particular market. Know the growth potentials, laws, rules, regulations, certification requirements, technical resources needed and where to obtain these, risks involved, and the competition.

The internet is awash with loads of information, and a little bit of research time could provide just about all the data you need to make an informed decision.

"It is not enough to take steps which may someday lead to a goal; each step must be itself a goal and a step likewise."

--------Johann Wolfgang Von Goethe

In fact, in many cases the time and efforts needed to come up with a business idea or product is much less than it would take to obtain some college degrees. It is really not that complicated! Yes, it is hard-work, but most people work hard anyway, usually for others, NOT FOR THEMSELVES unfortunately.

8. You must view and respect your time. Time is the most important resource that is usually taken for granted, and wasted. They say "time is money." If you have money you have time.

If your income generation process takes up the chunk of your time, then you are simply working for money. On the other hand, if the process takes less or none of your personal time, money is truly working for you. This is the most certain path to build wealth, and achieve the American dream.

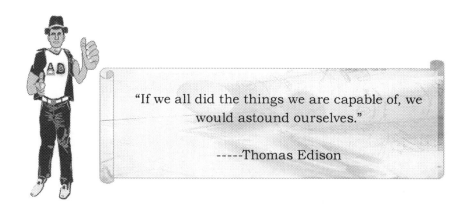

"If we all did the things we are capable of, we would astound ourselves."

-----Thomas Edison

THE "MADE IN CHINA" CRAZE ASSETS

Unless you have been surviving under a rock or you are simply a suckling born just yesterday, chances are, you have seen the "Made in China" tag on more goods than you can reckon. Who make or own these goods? How do they end up in our stores and homes?

Welcome to the world of capitalism! People just like you (yes, you!) own these goods. It's amazing how this works. Folks conduct feasibility studies to find products that are already being traded on the market. They then come out with different versions or better designs of the products and look for manufacturers in China through sites like Alibaba.com to make them for cheap.

Once they receive the consignments, they find stores, like Walmart, that are willing to carry the merchandise. They can also trade on eBay, Amazon etc. Soon, these products find their way to your home.

"Success is that old ABC- ability, breaks, and courage."

------Charles Luckman

THE POWER OF NETWORKING

Many people conceive ideas they hope and wish they could turn into economically viable products or services. Some take a few steps in an attempt to make it happen, but soon they are inundated with scary details and problems they have to deal with and surmount. Many people simply give up the effort altogether and just head back to work to collect paychecks for life.

The power of many is a force to reckon with, and if you want to get ahead in this economic era, the formation of networks and groups may be worth considering, given the following benefits they may present and perhaps many more.

People may come together in a group or network to brainstorm and come up with ideas they can turn into economically viable products or services. The diverse perspectives of the individuals in the group could provide the benefits of coming up with products or services which appeal to diverse consumer bases in the marketplace.

"There's only one thing that all the successful companies in the world have in common: None was started by one person."

-------Ernesto Sirolli

Cost-sharing by members of the group also has the potential to generate a much larger initial capital than a single individual could come up with. Pooling of resources by a sizable number of individuals to bear on an idea is a clear advantage that a group possesses over a single individual.

Risk-sharing to reduce individual exposure is another important advantage a group or network enjoys. With economic risks spread among members of the group, individuals could feel more secure with the knowledge that they might not lose everything in the event of total misadventure.

Task-sharing or task-distribution to bring different talents and perspectives to bear on an idea is an equally important leverage a group attains. A skill or expertise that the group would have had to spend money on may be obtained from some members of the group.

This could help the group conserve vital monetary resources which could be allocated to other areas as needed.

"Any change, even a change for the better, is always accompanied by drawbacks and discomfort."

-------Arnold Bennett

In this era of social media, there is a distinct advantage in the power of the crowd. Each member of the group knows many other people that the other members do not. This is an important resource which could be tapped into as needed for various purposes such as crowd-funding, product testing, marketing and promotion and so on.

WHAT IS A LIABILITY?

A liability simply means anything that causes a decrease in your bank account balance steadily and recurrently, say monthly. It could be a property, or something you mistakenly perceive to be an asset. Your home and your car are some of the distinctive properties which qualify as liabilities inasmuch as they are exclusively used for private purposes.

Let's consider a scenario where two people embark on a challenge to create the most wealth. They both earn the same amount of money monthly.

"Our dreams can come true if we have the courage to pursue them."

--------Walt Disney

One of them live in a smaller house with a $500 monthly mortgage, while the other lives in a $2000 monthly mortgaged house.

Assuming all other expenses are comparably equal, it's not too hard to appreciate which of the two would save the most money, and be able to invest the money saved. Whilst each of them has mortgage liabilities, one has more than the other. The same goes for a person who drives a gas-guzzler vehicle to work daily, and another who drives a gas-saver.

Again, since we all need roofs over our heads and means of transport to get around, those who find ways to cut costs on these liabilities are better off when it comes to saving money. Bear in mind, though, that saving money, alone, is NOT enough to become wealthy.

"The first requisite of success is the ability to apply your physical and mental energies to one problem without growing weary."

-----Thomas Edison

BASIC LIFE PRINCIPLES AND HABITS FOR SUCCESS

Lots of people have ideas they can turn into assets and bring them financial rewards and freedom. While they desire and wish they could just carry through and make it happen, there are certain hurdles they must clear in order to make their hopes and wishes come true. The following are some of life's basic principles they must adhere to.

FEAR OF FAILURE is the number one deterrent to success. The law of attraction, most people are familiar with, dictates that we attract to ourselves things that most dominate our thoughts. In other words, if you think you will succeed or fail you are right either way.

It is crucial that you rid yourself of the irrational fear of failure with adequate preparation, education and research on the issue at hand. This will pump up your confidence to succeed.

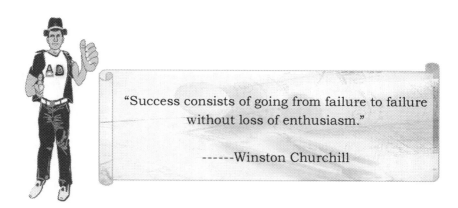

"Success consists of going from failure to failure without loss of enthusiasm."

------Winston Churchill

PROCRASTINATION ranks among the topmost reasons why projects stall. This is entirely self-evident. We go on kidding ourselves "I'll do it tomorrow," something that should have been done last year. The way out of this worriment is to lay out realistic goals with long and short term benchmarks, and BEGIN AT ONCE to put through the short term goals. I repeat! Make a list of these short-term goals and BEGIN AT ONCE to work on them, NOW.

It will likewise help to engage assistance from others to hold you accountable, to keep you on your toes as though your very life depends on it.

PERSISTENCE is key to getting any goals through. Unforeseen setbacks could easily frustrate the uninitiated into stalling or giving up efforts on, otherwise, good projects.

Don't tell yourself "things will get better." It won't! You (yes, you!) have to make things better.

"I'm convinced that about half of what separates the successful entrepreneurs from the non-successful ones is pure perseverance."

-------Steve Jobs

Things, by themselves, won't get any better than you left them. They wait for your next action.

ACTION is what separate dreamers from achievers. Without action your dreams remain dreams or nightmares as the case may be. Stop making up excuses and alibis and complaints. The world has no interest in your complaints and excuses, "show me the results, period!" Take action, even if they are baby steps. Soon, your destination will zoom clearer ahead and provide you steam to the finish line.

FAITH is key to making things happen. Faith in yourself and in a higher power, that is. Faith is a positive emotion.

Emotions are stronger than logic, which is why Jesus Christ said in the Sermon on the Mount that, if you have faith the size of a mustard seed you can move mountains. The mountains represent real problems, faith can move them.

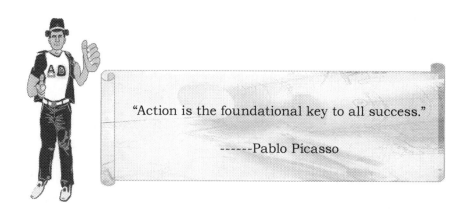

"Action is the foundational key to all success."

------Pablo Picasso

Faith and belief in a higher power are also the reason why every American president concludes every speech with "God bless the U.S.A."

Believing that there is a higher power you can count on to help provide answers or solution to seemingly insurmountable problems is quite assuring. All that is left is to take action with positive mental attitudes and relinquish doubtful mind-sets.

ENTHUSIASM about your idea or project is an important component to making it happen. Enthusiasm, like other emotions, is contagious.

Most projects require the cooperation and support of others other than yourself. To gain and secure such cooperation, your own level of enthusiasm will come into play. If you don't believe in your idea or project as much as to be so enthusiastic about it, then chances are, such cooperation and support will not be forthcoming

"Nothing great was ever achieved without enthusiasm."

-------Ralph Waldo Emerson

"Our greatest weakness lies in giving up. The most certain way to succeed is always to try just one more time."

--------Thomas Edison

"Experience teaches slowly, and at the cost of mistakes."

-----James A. Froude

"Failure is success if we learn from it."

----Malcolm Forbes

"Faith is the art of holding on to things your reason has once accepted, in spite of your changing moods."

----C.S. Lewis

PART THREE:

CONCLUSION AND SUGGESTIONS

IN CONCLUSION

"Old habits die hard." "Teach the child the way he should go so that he will not depart from it when he grows." These are some of the most important reasons why I recommend this book for readers nine (9) years and up. Most adults have habits that are very difficult to get around and overcome (even though it's not inconceivable to do so,) most kids don't. To give them a heads-up in the quest for financial freedom, you will help them a great deal by having them read this book over and over until the principles become ingrained.

Most people see problems and wonder or complain to the government to solve. Capitalists see problems as potential bonanzas for financial rewards. They begin thinking about HOW to solve the problem and get rewarded for their effort. They want to be the ones to solve problems, not the government.

"Contrary to the opinion of many people, leaders are not born. Leaders are made, and they are made by effort and hard work."

-----Vince Lombardi

My advice is that if you want to get ahead in this global economic landscape, and want same for your kids, begin by sniffing around to identify problems. You don't have to look far to unearth problems either. If you pay close attention to what problems you encounter, or have, you may realize that you are not alone with that problem. Others have noticed it too.

The high school student in England, I mentioned earlier, who designed the SUMMLY App came to this realization and decided to do something about it.

Mark Zuckerberg thought his friends and schoolmates needed a better means of sharing information and fun pictures, only to realize the entire world dig that stuff too. The resulting success is now history.

Don't get bogged down with technical details involved with the solutions and the capital required either.

"The person who gets the farthest is generally the one who is willing to do and dare. The sure-thing boat never gets far from shore."

-----Dale Carnegie

In many instances you can acquire technical information from academic and professional sources far cheaper than you imagine. For start-up capital, crowd funding (Kick Starter, for example) is here for the rescue. Systems, like the internet, are in place that can be harnessed to generate untold amount of wealth. You are limited ONLY by your own creativity and imagination.

Dream BIG! Mediocrity is pointless and unproductive. You are going to think anyway, you might as well think big. If you are going to speak, make a STATEMENT! Don't mumble, no one can hear you. Look, it doesn't require much more energy to think big. What are you going to dream up that could impact the world?

Activate and mobilize your creativity and imagination to advance the course of humanity. You will be handsomely rewarded financially for your endeavor and achievement. The American Dream is real and authentic. Begin to create assets NOW. Good luck to everyone!

"Happy are those who dream dreams and are ready to pay the price to make them come true."

-----Leon J. Suenes

INSPIRATIONAL QUOTATIONS

"I don't know the key to success, but the key to failure is trying to please everyone."

-----Bill Cosby

"In a gentle way, you can shake the world."

------Mohandas Gandhi

"Fall down seven times, get up eight."

----Japanese Proverb

"There is no impossibility to him who stands prepared to conquer every hazard. The fearful are the failing."

-----Sarah J. Hale

"The thing always happens that you really believe in; and the belief in a thing makes it happen."

-----Frank Lloyd Wright

"Vitality shows not only in the ability to persist, but in the ability to start over."

------- F. Scott Fitzgerald

"Winning isn't everything, but wanting to win is."

------Vince Lombardi.

"Along with success comes a reputation for wisdom."

-----Euripides

"Men's best successes come after their disappointments."

-----Henry Ward Beecher

"Yesterday does not equal tomorrow. Forget the past and move towards your goals."

------Tony Robbins

"A pessimist is one who makes difficulties of his opportunities, and an optimist is one who makes opportunities of his difficulties."

-------Harry Truman

"Real difficulties can be overcome; it is only the imaginary ones that are unconquerable."

-------Theodore N. Vail

"Great thoughts speak only to the thoughtful mind, but great actions speak to all mankind."

-------Emily P. Bissell

"The most important single ingredient in the formula of success is knowing how to get along with people."

--------Theodore Roosevelt

"Years from now you will be more disappointed by the things that you didn't do than by the ones you did. So throw off the bowlines. Sail away from the safe harbor. Catch the trade winds in your sails. Explore. Dream. Discover."

-------H. Jackson Brown, Jr.

"People who are crazy enough to think they can change the world, are the ones who do."

-------Rob Siltanen

"You must be the change that you wish to see in the world."

-------Mohandas Karamchand Gandhi

"In matters of style, swim with the current; in matters of principle, stand like a rock."

-------Thomas Jefferson

"The pessimist sees difficulty in every opportunity. The optimist sees the opportunity in every difficulty."

-------Winston Churchill

"Obstacles are those frightful things you see when you take your eyes off the goal."

-------Henry Ford

"Don't worry about failure; you only have to be right once."

--------Drew Houston

"Not all those who wander are lost."

-------J. R. R. Tolkien

"It is a common experience that a problem difficult at night is resolved in the morning after a committee of sleep has worked on it."

--------John Steinbeck

"In order to succeed, your desire for success should be greater than your fear of failure."

--------Bill Cosby

"The man who has confidence in himself gains the confidence of others."

---------Hasidic Proverb

"We learn wisdom from failure much more than success. We often discover what we will do, by finding out what we will not do."

----Samuel Smiles

"Success is the good fortune that comes from aspiration, desperation, perspiration and inspiration."

------Evan Esar

"Having once decided to achieve a certain task, achieve it at all cost of tedium and distaste. The gain in self-confidence of having accomplished a tiresome labor is immense."

-----Arnold Bennett

"Significance in life doesn't come from status, because you can always find somebody who's got more than you..... It does not come from salary. It comes from serving."

--------Rick Warren

"Defeat is not the worst of failures. Not to have tried is the true failure."

-------George Edward Woodberry

"Belief in oneself is one of the most important bricks in building any successful venture."

--------Lydia M. Child

"If you have built castles in the air, your work need not be lost; that is where they should be. Now put the foundations under them."

-------Henry David Thoreau

"Do not let what you cannot do interfere with what you can do."

-------John Wooden

"What counts is not necessarily the size of the dog in the fight–it's the size of the fight in the dog."

-------Dwight D. Eisenhower

"It is surmounting difficulties that makes heroes."

-----Louis Pasture

"Nothing in life is to be feared; it is only to be understood."

----Marie Curie

"Dreams are today's answers to tomorrow's questions."

-------Edgar Cayce

"Believe with all your heart that you will do what you were made to do."

----Orison Swett Marden

"Nothing happens unless first a dream."

-----Carl Sandburg

"The beginning is the most important part of the work."

-------Plato

"Follow your honest convictions, and stay strong."

----William Thackeray

"There is no failure except in no longer trying.

--------Elbert Hubbard

"Joy is the will which labors, which overcomes obstacles, which knows triumph."

-----William Butler Yeats

"Courage is not simply one of the virtues, but the form of every virtue at the testing point."

----C.S. Lewis

"The only peace, the only security, is in fulfilment."

----Henry Miller

"Always do what you are afraid to do."

------Ralph Waldo Emerson

"Well begun is half done."

----Aristotle

"A man who wants to lead the orchestra must turn his back on the crowd."

---Max Lucado

"The ability to convert ideas into things is the secret to outward success."

-----Henry Ward Beecher

"They conquer who believe they can."

-------John Dryden

"Success doesn't come to you.....you go to it."

-----Marva Collins

"Every artist was first an amateur."

-----Ralph Waldo Emerson

"Success has a simple formula: do your best and people may like it."

------Sam Ewing

"In order to succeed, you must be willing to fail."

-----Author Unknown

"To climb steep hills requires a slow pace at first."

----- William Shakespeare

"Be less curious about people and more curious about ideas."

------Marie Curie

"We cannot do everything at once, but we can do something at once."

-----Calvin Coolidge

"Self trust is the first secret of success."

---Ralph Waldo Emerson

"If you care at all, you will get results. If you care enough, you will get incredible results."

--------Jim Rohn

"He who does not tire, tires adversity."

------Author Unknown

"If your actions inspire others to dream more, learn more, do more and become more, you are a leader."

------John Quincy Adams.

"Sow an act, and you reap a habit; sow a habit, and you reap a character; sow a character, and you reap a destiny."

-----George Dana Boardman

"Action, not words, are the ultimate results of leadership."

-----Bill Owens

"The great artist and thinker are the simplifiers."

-------Henri Frederic Amiel

"In order to succeed you must fail, so that you know what not to do the next time."

------Anthony J. D'Angelo

"Develop success from failures. Discouragement and failure are two of the surest stepping stones to success."

--------Dale Carnegie

"The beginning is the most important part of the work."

-------Plato

"What lies behind us and what lies before us are tiny matters compared to what lies within us."

--------Walt Emerson

"Obstacles cannot crush me, every obstacle yields to stern resolve."

-------Leonardo da Vinci

"Inspiration and genius--one and the same."

------Victor Hugo

"Goals are the fuel in the furnace of achievement."

------Brian Tracy

"All of the great leaders have had one characteristic in common: it was the willingness to confront unequivocally the major anxiety of their people in their time."

-----John Kenneth Galbraith

"The power of imagination makes us infinite."

----John Muir

"However long the night, the dawn will break."

------African Proverb

"If you would create something, you must be something."

------Johann Wolfgang Von Goethe

"The highest reward for a man's toil is not what he gets for it, but what he becomes by it."   -----John Ruskin

If you can dream it, you can do it."

------Walt Disney

"Storms make oaks take roots."

----Proverb

"All life is an experiment. The more experiment you make the better."

----Ralph Waldo Emerson

"God gives every bird a worm, but He does not throw it into the nest."

-----Swedish Proverb

"It is hard to fail, but it is worse never to have tried to succeed."

------Theodore Roosevelt

"Change and growth take place when a person has risked himself and dares to become involved with experimenting with his own life."

--------Herbert Otto

"Believe in yourself and there will come a day when others will have no choice but to believe with you."

--------Cynthia Kersey

"It is not enough to take steps which may someday lead to a goal; each step must be itself a goal and a step likewise."

--------Johann Wolfgang Von Goethe

"All men who have achieved great things have been great dreamers."

------Orison Swett Marden

"Every failure brings with it the seed of an equivalent success."

------Napoleon Hill

"Diligence is the mother of good luck."

--------American Proverb

"Do what you can, with what you have, where you are."

-------Theodore Roosevelt

"Heaven never helps the man who will not act."

-----Sophocles

"People need dreams, there's as much nourishment in them as food."

------Dorothy Gilman

"Do not go where the path may lead, go instead where there is no path and leave a trail."

-----Ralph Waldo Emerson

"A successful man is one who can lay a firm foundation with bricks others have thrown at him."

----David Brinkley

"People rarely succeed unless they have fun in what they are doing."

-------Dale Carnegie

"Our greatest glory consists not in never falling, but rising every time we fall."

--------Oliver Goldsmith

"Motivation is the fuel, necessary to keep the human engine running."

-------Zig Ziglar

"Life's most persistent and urgent question is, 'what are you doing for others?"

------Martin Luther King, Jr.

"If there is no struggle, there is no progress."

----Frederick Douglass

"Success is often the result of taking a misstep in the right direction."

----Al Bernstein

"What you get by reaching your destination is not as nearly as important as what you will become by reaching your destination."

------Zig Ziglar

"Honor bespeaks worth. Confidence begets trust. Service brings satisfaction. Cooperation proves the quality of leadership."

------James Cash Penney

"Good leadership consist of showing average people how to do the work of superior people."

----------John D. Rockefeller

"A good objective of leadership is to help those who are doing poorly to do well and to help those who are doing well to do even better."

------Jim Rohn

"Flaming enthusiasm, backed up by horse sense and persistence, is the quality that most frequently makes for success."

---Dale Carnegie

"Our greatest glory consists not in never falling, but rising every time we fall."

---------Oliver Goldsmith

"Anyone who has never made a mistake has never tried anything new."

----Albert Einstein

"Believe you can and you are halfway there."

----------Theodore Roosevelt

"Do not pray for easy lives. Pray to be stronger men."

--------John F. Kennedy

"Leadership is unlocking people's potential to become better."

------Bill Bradley

"Things do not happen. Things are made to happen."

---John F. Kennedy

"I've failed over and over and over again in my life and that is why I succeed."

----Michael Jordan

"There is little you can learn from doing nothing."

----Zig Ziglar

"Keep steadily before you the fact that all true success depends at last upon YOURSELF."

--------Theodore T. Hunger

"Leadership requires the courage to make decisions that will benefit the next generation."

------Alan Autry

"The best way to predict the future is to create it."

-----Peter F. Drucker

"Find a meaningful need and fulfil it better than anyone else. This is success."

----Author Unknown.

"I failed my way to success."

-----Thomas Edison

"Courage is resistance to fear, mastery of fear, not absence of fear."

-----Mark Twain

"The ladder of success is best climbed by stepping on the rungs of opportunity."

--------Ayn Rand

"Faith has to do with things that are not seen and hope with things that are not at hand."

----Saint Thomas Aquinas

"A man of courage is also full of faith."

-------Marcus Tullius Cicero

"What happens is not as important as how you react to what happens."

---Thaddeus Golas

"Find a meaningful need and fulfill it better than anyone else. This is success."

----Author Unknown.

"You are happiest while you are making the greatest contribution."

---Robert F. Kennedy

"An obstacle is often a stepping stone."

-------William Prescott

"The surest way not to fail is to determine to succeed."

----Richard Brinkley Sheridan

"What the minds can conceive and believe, it can achieve."

-----Napoleon Hill

"The function of leadership is to produce more leaders, not more followers."

--------Ralph Nader

"The purpose of life is a life of purpose."

----Robert Byrne

"You cannot dream yourself into a character; you must hammer and forge yourself one."

-----Henry David Thoreau

"I believe that the true road to preeminent success in any line is to make yourself master of that line."

-------Andrew Carnegie

"You will never do anything in this world without courage. It is the greater quality of the mind next to honor."

-----Aristotle

"Self trust is the first secret of success."

---Ralph Waldo Emerson

"Faith is taking the first step even when you don't see the whole staircase."

-----Martin Luther King, Jr.

"Little minds are tamed and subdued by misfortunes; but great minds rise above them."

-----Washington Irving

"One who fears failure limits his activities. Failure is only the opportunity to more intelligently begin again."

----Henry Ford

"What would life be if we had no courage to attempt anything?"

------Vincent Van Gogh

"Nothing will ever be attempted if all possible objections must first be overcome."

---Samuel Johnson

"If we do not plant knowledge when young, it will give us no shade when we are old."

------Lord Chesterfield

"DREAM NO SMALL DREAMS FOR THEY HAVE NO POWER TO MOVE THE HEARTS OF MEN."

------Johann Wolfgang von Goethe

NOTES

AUTHOR'S NOTES

EXTRACTS FROM A MOTIVATIONAL ADDRESS IN NEW YORK

THEME: The Fruit of the Holy Spirit:

Exploring God's Resources for Growth and Development

Bring the whole tithe into the storehouse, that there may be food in my house.

Test me in this, says The Lord Almighty, and see if I will not throw open the floodgates of Heaven and pour out so much blessing that you will not have room enough for it. (The English Standard Version says: until there is no more need)

I will prevent pests from devouring your crops, and the vines in your fields will not cast their fruit, says The Lord Almighty.

Then all the nations will call you blessed, for yours will be a delightful land, says The Lord Almighty. Malachi 3:10

The Promise....Access the Promise. We all have needs, and God knows we do; health, relationships, financial etc.

2.   The Faith......Test me in this, with Faith

3.   Knowledge......Hosea 4:6 For lack of knowledge, my people perish

Action.....Test me in this.....by Faith in Action. ......It's not enough to have Faith, you have to Act on the Faith........knowing "I can do ALL THINGS through Christ which strengthens me." ....Philippians 4:13

God helps those who help THEMSELVES. Acts 17:11. The key word is "THEMSELVES."

Helping your employer doesn't necessarily mean that you are helping YOURSELF. Your employer is helping "HIMSELF," and asking God to help him. You are simply a tool, a replaceable tool of your employer. The big question is, when are you going to step out in FAITH to help YOURSELF so that God can help you as He has promised? The thing that moves God to act on our behalf is FAITH, not FEAR.

The worker who helps the farmer and get paid has no more share in a bountiful harvest. His portion is the same paycheck even when the harvest is 10 times the normal yield. The farmer planted his seeds and prayed to God to send the rain, sunshine etc. at the right times.

God fulfilled His promises, and now there is bountiful harvest. The farmer owes you no more than your paycheck.

Your SEED, which is your tithe, is what God multiplies. Your FAITH, however, is the reason He multiplies your seed. The key word here is "YOUR SEED." Not your employer's seed or someone else's, but "YOUR SEED". You have to sow YOUR SEED, then you can lay a claim on God's promise when you act in FAITH.

Be ready to step out in faith. Find your very OWN calling, and ask God for help in fulfilling it. Then work as hard as you work for your employer and see if God will not throw open the flood gates Heaven and pour out so much blessing that you will not have room enough for it as He has promised.

The Lord will open to you His good treasury, the heavens, to give the rain to your land in its season and to bless all the work of YOUR HANDS. And you shall lend to many nations, but YOU SHALL NOT BORROW.

And The Lord will make YOU the HEAD and NOT the tail, and you shall only go up and not down, IF you obey the commandments of God, which I command you today, being careful to DO them....

......Deuteronomy 28:12-13

Matthew 7:7-11 "Ask, and it will be given to you; seek, and you will find; knock, and it will be opened to you. For everyone who asks receives, and the one who seeks finds, and the one who knock it will be opened. Or which one of you, if his son asks him for bread, will give him a stone? Or if he asks for fish, will give him a serpent?

If you then, who are evil, know how to give good gifts to your children, how much more will your Father who is in heaven give good things to those who ask him!"

Christ has demonstrated this before in Matthew 14:13. He took a little boy's lunch of 5 loaves of bread and 2 fish as seed, and multiplied it to feed over 5K men, and still had 12 basketfuls of leftovers (until there was no more need)

The same God is still doing great things. You have to step out in FAITH and ask for His help, His blessing, and His hand in it. He will do it according to your FAITH. Christ told the woman that was bleeding "YOUR FAITH has healed you."
....

..............Mark 5:34

Without faith no one can please God: - Hebrews 11:6. With faith, you can move mountains: - Matthew 17:6.

Mountains are problems, hurdles, impediments etc. Things that block your way from reaching your destination. You can move them with faith.

When Peter stepped out of the boat and begun walking on the water, in Matthew 14:22, he did so by faith. That whole passage is there for our benefit. That was a demonstration of FAITH IN ACTION.

The fact that Peter begun to sink when he started looking at the treacherous roaring seas is also teaching us to keep our eyes on Christ to get us through any frightening situation. Do not take your eyes off of Him. But you have to take action. You have to step out in faith.

When Christ stepped forward to die for our sins, knowing that in three days His father will resurrect Him, and that was the ultimate demonstration of FAITH.

I pray that The Lord strengthens our faith in Him so we can step out in faith to possess our possessions so that we can all share our testimonies to glorify His name. In Jesus name we pray. Amen!

NOTES

NOTES

NOTES

NOTES

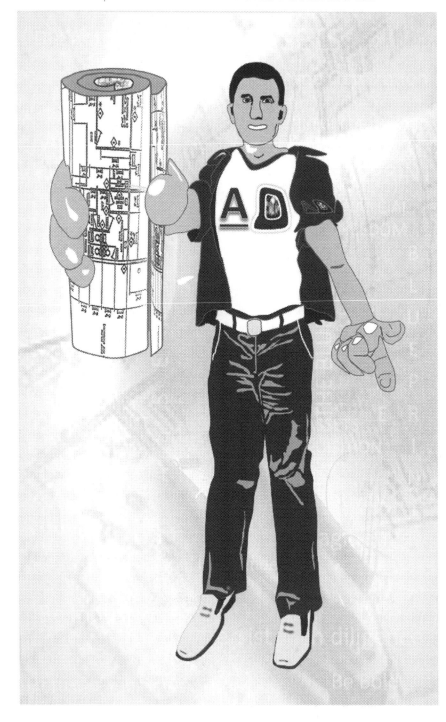

A must-read, insightful blueprint to fulfilling your dreams and potentials of becoming financially emancipated.

This book is a culmination of 4 years of extensive and meticulous research to uncover why some people do so well in the capitalist economy while the vast majority struggle to make ends meet. My quest was to discover answers to these elusive questions about the few who are doing so handsomely well: What do they know? What do they do differently?

The research results were a total shock to my very core. I simply could not believe how uncomplicated it really is to create wealth and live the American Dream. "For lack of knowledge my people perish."---Hosea 4:6.

Education is THE KEY to success in any endeavor. Financial Education is THE KEY to financial success, and in the current globalized economic environment, everyone needs that in addition to their degrees, diplomas, and professional training. That need is essential and cardinal now than ever before. This book provides the entire Financial Education package, which would help readers expand their means rather than just managing their current, often meagre means, in an easy-to-understand step-by-step approach towards Financial Freedom.

The
American Dream
DECLASSIFIED

◆

Frank PN Adjei-Mensah

author**HOUSE**®